God gave Adam the job of naming all the creatures in the Garden of Eden.
Can you find fifteen white flowers in this picture?
Look up the story of Adam and Eve in the garden in Genesis 2:8–25.

A serpent persuaded Eve to eat the forbidden fruit in the Garden of Eden.
Which two serpents here are exactly the same?
Read the story in Genesis 3:1–6.

Eve ate the forbidden fruit in the Garden of Eden.
Can you find nine hidden fruits here? What is coiled around the tree?
Read the story in Genesis 3:1–6.

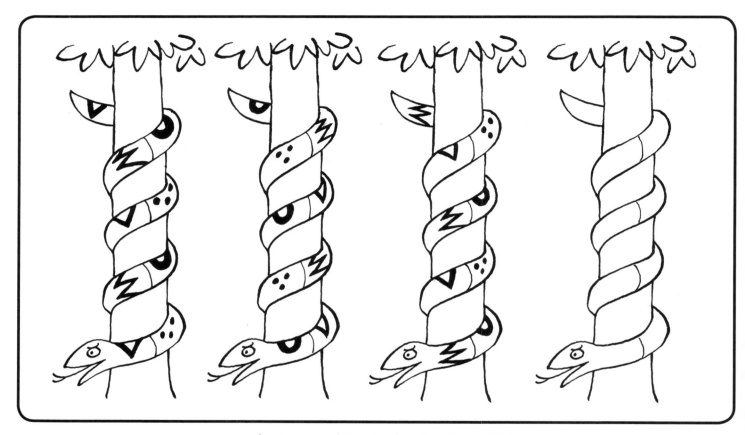

A snake tempted Eve in the Garden of Eden.
The pattern moves up this snake. Can you complete the last picture correctly?
Read Genesis 3:1–24.

God told Noah to collect together two of every kind of animal. He was going to save them from the flood that was coming. Find the odd one out in this picture.
Look in Genesis 6:21 to discover what God also told Noah to put in the ark.

Noah collected up two of each kind of bird and animal.
Find the right lines to match up these pairs.
This story is in Genesis 6:9–22.

Complete this picture of the animals marching into Noah's ark two by two,
using felt-tips, paints, or crayons.
Read Genesis 6:10 to find the names of Noah's sons.

The enormous boat that Noah built was like a floating zoo.
Find ten differences between these pictures.
You can read the story of Noah's ark in Genesis 6:1 – 9:17.

When the great flood was over, who carried an olive branch to Noah?
Shade in the dotted areas to find out.
Now read Genesis 8:1–12.

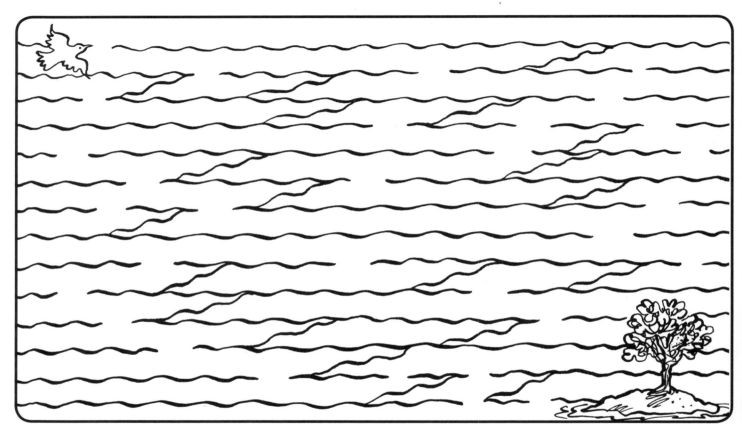

Noah sent out a dove from the ark. Help the dove find its way
to the olive tree without crossing any waves in the water.
You can read this story in Genesis 8:6–12.

The rain finally stopped after forty days, but the flood water took a long time to go down. What did the dove carry back to Noah in its beak? Which outline exactly matches the finished drawing of the bird? *Read Genesis 8:11.*

Poor Joseph was sold by his brothers. Find all the deliberate mistakes in this picture. You can read this story in your Bible. *Read Genesis 37:12–37.* Which brother tried to stop Joseph from being taken away?

When he was still a baby, Moses' mother hid him in a basket on the River Nile.
Which two ducks in the river are exactly the same?
You can read the story of baby Moses in Exodus 2:1–10.

When he grew up, Moses ran away from Egypt. He worked for a time as a shepherd in the desert.
Where are his sheep? Draw some sheep and finish the picture with crayons.
Read this story in Exodus 2:15–25.

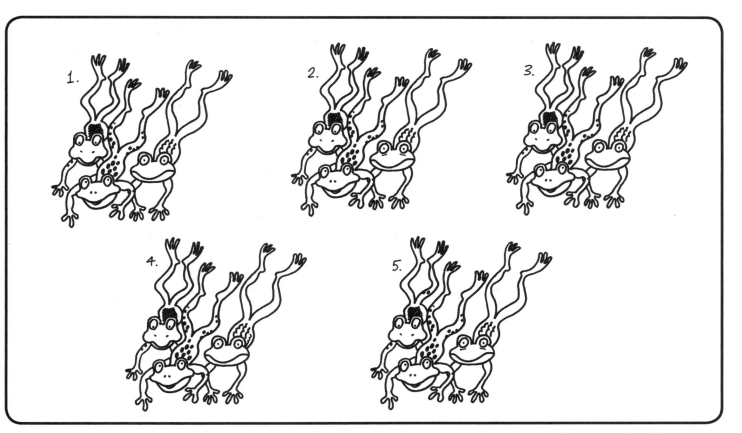

In the time of Moses, God sent many terrible plagues to Egypt. One time, thousands of frogs spread everywhere. Which two of these groups of frogs are exactly the same?
You can read about the plague of frogs in Exodus 8:1–14.

God was showing his power to the king of Egypt. He sent pesky frogs everywhere.
Find ten differences between these two pictures.
You can read about the frogs in Egypt in Exodus 8:1–15.

Another time, God sent thousands of filthy flies that flew everywhere in Egypt. He wanted the king of Egypt to let his people go free. Circle all ten differences between these two pictures. *Read about this plague in Exodus 8:20–30.*

Later all the cattle in Egypt caught a terrible disease. But still the king of Egypt wouldn't let the Hebrews go free. Which two pictures are exactly the same?
You can find this story in Exodus 9:1–7.

The Hebrews finally escaped from Egypt. They walked for days in the desert.
God sent birds called quails for his people to eat. Which two quails here are exactly the same?
Read this story in Exodus chapter 16.

Moses climbed Mount Sinai to meet with God. He was away a long time.
Join up the dots to see the idol that the Hebrews danced around while Moses was away.
Read Exodus 32:1–4.

The Hebrews bowed down to worship the golden calf they had made.
The artist has made a lot of mistakes here. Put a circle around each mistake.
Read Exodus 32:1–35. Where did they get the gold to make their golden calf?

Join up the dots. What is giving Balaam's donkey such a fright?
You can find this story in Numbers 2:1–35.
What was special about Balaam's donkey?

Samson was a very strong man because of his very long hair. Once he killed a lion with just his bare hands! How many silly mistakes can you find here?
Read this story in Judges 14:5–6.

Samson was strong and brave. One day he killed a lion that attacked him.
Find ten differences between these two pictures of Samson and the lion.
Read this story in your Bible in Judges 14:1–9. What did Samson find later on the lion?

Ruth went to gather wheat for her mother-in-law Naomi in fields that belonged to Boaz.
Can you find twenty harvest mice hidden in this picture?
Look up the story of Ruth working in the fields in Ruth 2.

David was a shepherd boy when Samuel told him that one day he would become king of Israel.
Put a circle around all the differences you can find between these two pictures.
Read this story in 1 Samuel chapter 16.

In the time of David, dangerous animals lived in the countryside.
What creature is trying to attack David's sheep here? Join up the dots to find out.
You can read this story in 1 Samuel 17:34–37.

Here are some of David's sheep.
Which outline exactly fits the finished drawing of a sheep?
Read about David in 1 Samuel chapter 16.

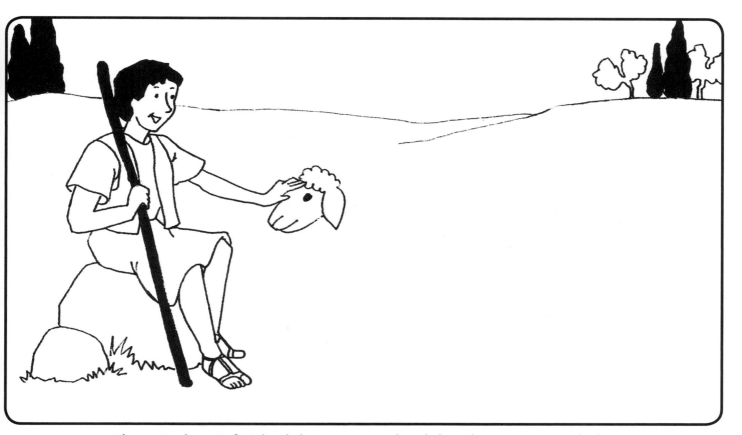

The artist hasn't finished drawing David with his sheep: can you help?
Complete the picture with your pencil, crayons, or felt-tips.
Read the "shepherd psalm", Psalm 23.

When David became king, he ordered priests to bring the Holy Ark of God to Jerusalem.
Join up the dots to find out who pulled the cart towards Jerusalem.
Read about David dancing in 2 Samuel 6:12–15.

Elijah was hiding in the desert. He was running away from wicked King Ahab.
Join up the dots to find out who brought him food.
You can find this story in 1 Kings 17:1–7.

31

Daniel has been thrown into a pit by the king of Babylon.
Why is he looking a bit scared? Join up the dots to find out.
You can find this story in Daniel 6:16–23.

God sent an angel to close the mouths of the lions that were in the pit with Daniel.
How many matching pairs of lions can you find here? Can you find four?
Read the story of Daniel and the lions in Daniel 6:16–23.

33

Daniel was thrown into a den full of lions. King Darius was pleased that God's angel shut the lions' mouths and Daniel was kept safe. Fill in this picture with your crayons or felt-tips. *Read this story in Daniel 6:19–23.*

Jonah was in a boat, trying to escape from God. A great storm came and the sailors threw him overboard. Join up the dots. What's happening to Jonah?
You can find this story in Jonah 1:1–17.

A huge fish swallowed Jonah. God sent the fish to save him from drowning.
Which outline exactly matches the finished picture?
Read Jonah 2:10. Why did the fish swim to land?

Here are two pictures of the great fish that swallowed Jonah.
How many differences can you find? *You can read this story in Jonah 1:1–17.*
How many days was Jonah inside the fish?

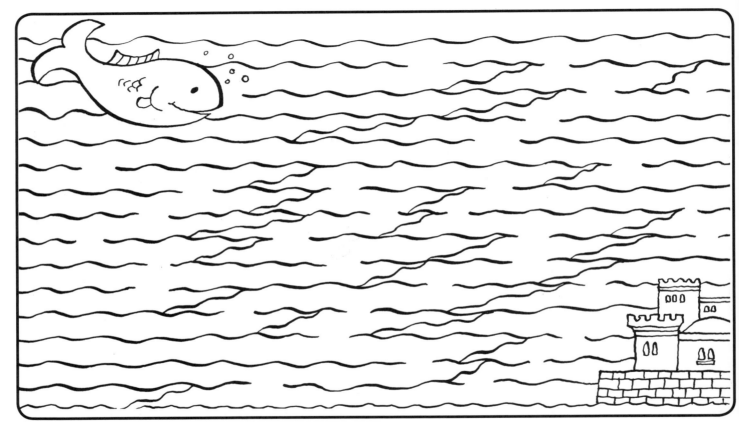

This enormous fish swallowed Jonah. Can you find your way through the sea
to the city of Nineveh, so Jonah can escape? Don't cross any waves!
Read the story in Jonah 1:1–17.

After three days the great fish spat out Jonah onto the seashore.
What is Jonah saying here? Fill in his speech bubble.
Read Jonah 2:1–10 to help you.

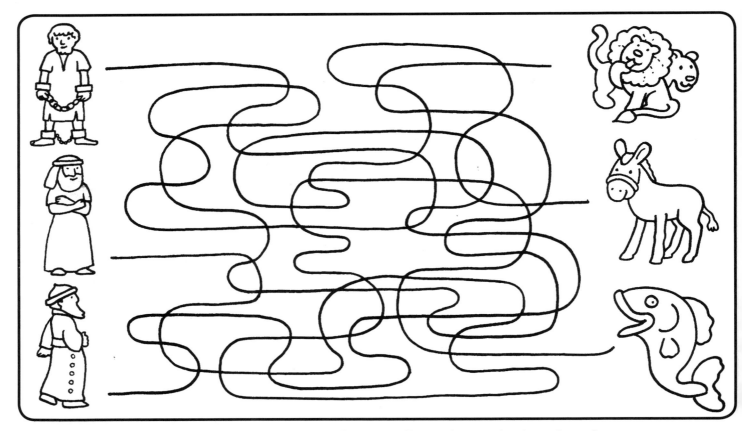

Daniel, Balaam, and Jonah were all prophets who loved God.
Match up Daniel, Balaam, and Jonah with the correct animal.
You can read about Balaam's journey in Numbers 22:22–35.

When Joseph and Mary arrived in Bethlehem, they found there was no room for them at the inn. Complete this picture of the stable where Jesus was born by drawing some animals, a door, and some windows. *You can read about Jesus' birth in Luke 2:7.*

Baby Jesus was born in a stable in the town of Bethlehem.
Which picture of the stable is the odd one out?
Read the story in Luke 2:6–7.

After Jesus was born, shepherds came to see him. Who told the shepherds where to find baby Jesus? How many mistakes has the artist made here? Put a circle around every mistake. *This story is in Luke 2:8–20.*

There was perhaps a donkey sheltering in the stable where Jesus was born.
Which box has all the pieces needed to make up the donkey?
Read about the stable in Bethlehem in Luke 2:1–7.

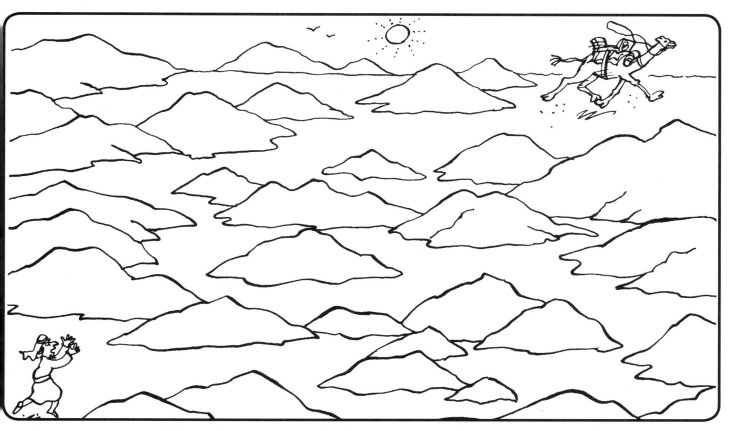

Wise men journeyed from the East to visit baby Jesus. One of the wise men has lost his camel.
Help him follow his camel through the desert maze. (Don't cross any little hills.)
You can read about the wise men in Matthew 2:1–2.

Anna was a very old lady when she saw baby Jesus in the Temple. How happy she was!
She had been waiting many years. Can you find eleven doves in this picture?
Look up the story of Anna's joy in Luke 2:36–38.

Joseph and Mary took Jesus to Jerusalem for a special festival. But they lost him. At last they found him, talking with priests in the Temple. Can you find eight fish hidden in this picture? *Read this story in Luke 2:45–48.* What is Mary saying to Jesus?

Jesus called two brothers to follow him. What was the name of the lake where they were fishing? Find all the deliberate mistakes in this picture. *You can read this story in Matthew 4:18–20.*

One time Jesus told his friends how to catch more fish. What did he say?
Read this story in Luke 5:1–11. Who does this boat belong to?
Can you find all the artist's deliberate mistakes here?

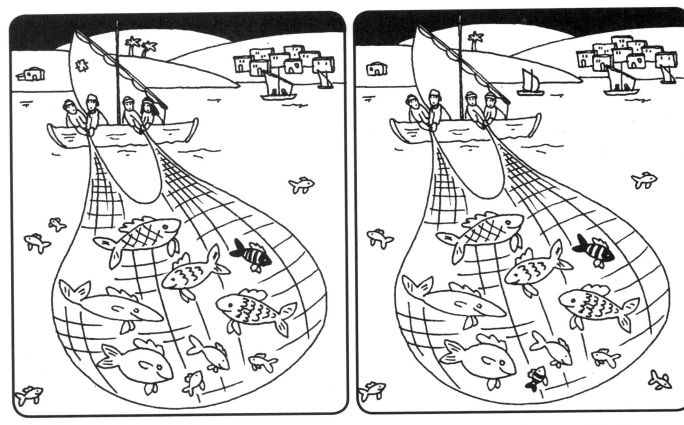

These fishermen are using a dragnet to catch all sorts of fish in the Sea of Galilee.
Read what Jesus said about a dragnet in Matthew 13:47–50.
Now find ten differences between the two pictures.

Jesus once told a story about a good shepherd and a lost sheep. Here is the shepherd with his sheep. How many differences can you spot between the two pictures?
Read John 10:14 to find out what Jesus called himself.

It's the end of the day and the shepherd is counting his sheep.
How many funny mistakes can you find here? Do you think the shepherd has lost any sheep?
Read Luke 15:4–5 to find out what the shepherd did when a sheep went missing.

One of the shepherd's sheep went missing.
Here are seven of his sheep. Which is the odd one out?
Read Luke 15:4–5 to find out about the good shepherd.

The shepherd went out on a dark night to find his lost sheep.
When the shepherd got home with the sheep he called together his friends to celebrate.
Read Luke 15:5–6. Now fill in the shepherd's speech bubble.

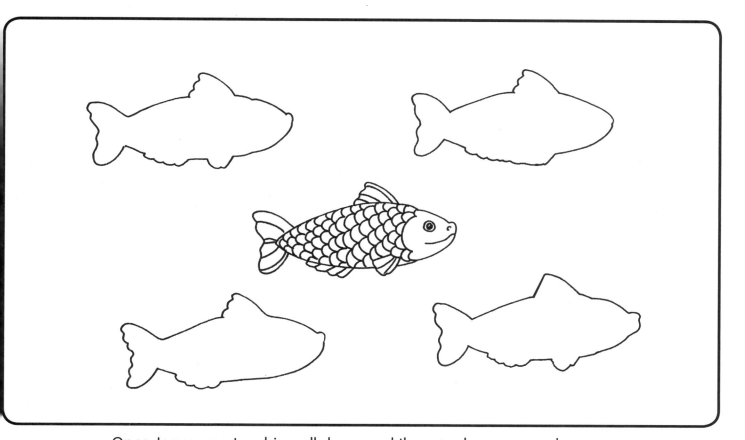

Once Jesus was teaching all day – and the people grew very hungry.
Only one boy had any food. This boy had five small loaves and two little fish.
Which outline exactly fits the finished drawing of a fish? *Read this story in John 6:5–15.*

Jesus told a story about a shepherd who separated his sheep from his goats.
Find all ten differences between the two pictures.
You can read what Jesus said about sheep and goats in Matthew 25:31–43.

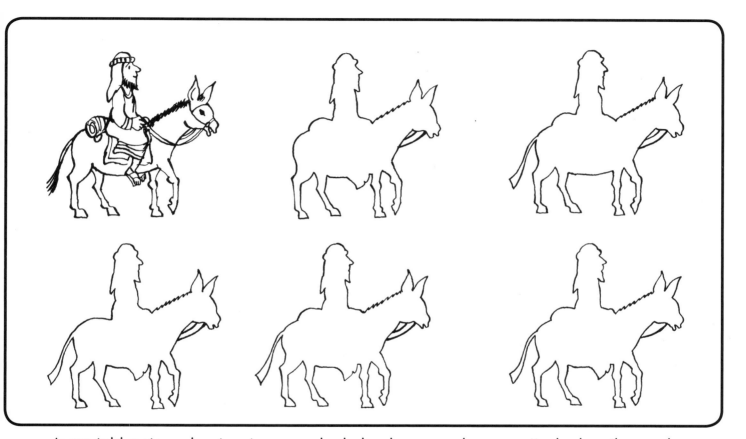

Jesus told a story about a stranger who helped a man who was attacked on the road. Here is a picture of the man with his donkey. Which outline exactly fits the finished picture?
Read this story in Luke 10:25–37.

Jesus told a story about a son who left home. When he ran out of money
he found a job. Join up the dots to find out what his job was.
You can find this story in Luke 15:11–31.

Here are two pictures of the son who left home, feeding pigs.
Put a circle around all the differences you can find between them.
Read this story in Luke 15:14–16.

Here is the lost son looking after the pigs.
The artist hasn't finished the drawing. Complete the pigs and use felt-tips to fill in the picture.
Read the whole story in Luke 15:11–32.

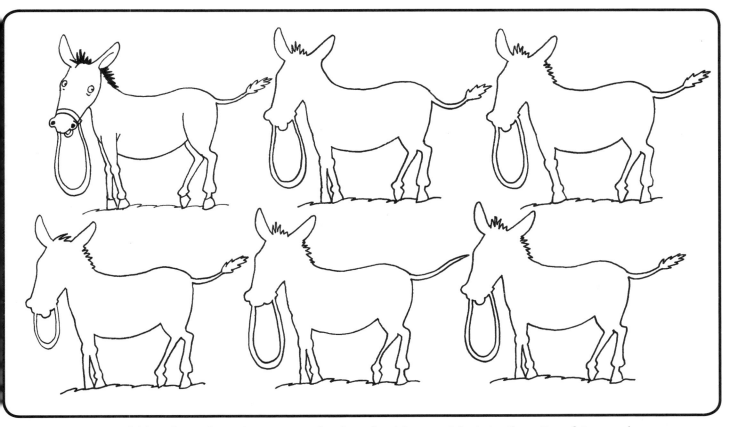

Jesus told his friends to borrow a donkey for him to ride into the city of Jerusalem.
Which outline exactly fits the finished donkey? Now complete all the donkeys.
You can read this story in Matthew 21:1–7.

One sad night soldiers took Jesus prisoner. Peter swore that he didn't know Jesus.
Then he heard a cockerel crow. Can you find all the differences between these two pictures?
Read Mark 14:71–72.

A cockerel crowed after Peter said he didn't know Jesus.
Which box has all the pieces needed to make the complete cockerel?
Read the story in John 18:15–18, 25–27.

Saul journeyed to Damascus to arrest Christians living there. On the way, Jesus spoke to him. Can you find all the differences between these two pictures of Saul? *Read this story in Acts 9:1–18.* What is happening to him here?